FLATLINE HORIZON

2018

FIRST EDITION, XXXX

Flatline Horizon
© 2018 by Don Stinson

ISBN 978-1-7323935-2-3

Except for fair use in reviews and/or scholarly
considerations, no part of this book may be reproduced,
performed, recorded, or otherwise transmitted without the
written consent of the author and
the permission of the publisher.

Cover Art
Moon Rising Over Walkway
© 2016 by Ken Crowder

Author Photo
@ 2018 by Pamela Stinson

MONGREL EMPIRE PRESS
NORMAN, OK

Online catalogue: www.mongrelempire.org

This publisher is a proud member of

COUNCIL OF LITERARY MAGAZINES & PRESSES
w w w . c l m p . o r g

Contents

The Old Country	1
Witch Season	2
Ballad of a Moment	3
It's All Over Now	4
An Old Southern Tale	5
A Previously Unreported Incident	6
As a Bone	7
Deletion	8
Melancholia	9
Nebraska, May	10
Love and Death in the Natural Order of Things	11
Skid	12
Liberation	13
Two Hours West of Tulsa	14
California	15
The Metaphysics of Prairie	20
Pineapples	21
In the Kiamichis	22
Oklahoma Panhandle	23
Mentone, California, 1969	24
The Woman at the Port Angeles Cemetery	25
Lizard King	26
On Sparrowhawk Mountain	28
Pastoral	29
Florence, 2015	30
Travelogue	31
Fame, Fame, Fame, Fame	32
As in Certain Paintings of Paul Klee	33
Cinema Noir	34
Blank Document	35
Picasso Kite	36
Them Blues	37
Alzheimer's	38
Life Insurance	39
Mors Praematura	40
Sawdust Man	41

The Something Else	42
On Three Hats of My Father's	44
At the Gospel Singing	45
Never Pills	47
Sometimes	49
Agnostic Stanzas	50
Of Winter and Ordinary Time	51
A Matter of Fact	52
One Reason the Agnostic Still Prays	53
On the Eastern Front	54
Winter Solo	55
Winter Solstice 2016	56
Fog	59
Black and Green	60
Mirrors	61
64% of a Sonnet on the Eternal Theme	64
Rising Green	65
Vegetation	66
Tighter	67
Memory Upon Waking	68
Bipolar	69

FLATLINE HORIZON

DON STINSON

*For my teachers and mentors—
Joan Shaddox Isom, Mark Cox, and
Dr. Lisa Lewis.*

For my children—Caleb, Ethan, and Emily.

Above all, for Pam.

The Old Country

There, they fold the days neatly away
like freshly-laundered, ironed sheets.

The women are tall, but the men are taller.
Morals flourish between corn's straight rows.

The sun lingers longer than anywhere else
because the girls are so beautiful.

Neighbors raise each other's barns
in timed competitions for *schnapps*.

Each genealogy is read in the face,
births, baptisms, weddings, funerals.

The steeples outnumber the shadows,
though folks avoid the full moon's glare.

There, your passport is stamped in blood.

Witch Season

The cart's wheels,
caked with muck,
crunch over limbs
that snap like bones.

The devil-whores
keen and wail
at the very sight
of the sacred rood.

We herd them in, and
the examinations begin.
Some float.
Some don't.

The red-tressed one,
with the cat scratches
across her vile back?
She burned quite blue.

Afterwards, life resumed.
We planted by the moon,
and could hide in the corn,
which rose like dying curses.

Ballad of a Moment

I've seen death with its flashlight
trolling the dark waters
at the base of your spine.
You remain closed.

All around you the worlds
pause in their revolutions
as wonderful birds whirl
sadly through the falling leaves.

A moment once arrived,
dropped its bags, glanced about,
dissolved through one of
the innumerable cracks in the floor.

Long autumn brushes winter's coat.
Summer's lost in closeted slumber.
The beam slides over your shoulder,
somehow now far behind you.

It's All Over Now

Past the dirt lane,
past the sycamore,
past the green house,
past the open door,

Past the black hearse,
past the tall stone,
past the memory,
past all alone,

Past yesterday,
past today, tomorrow,
past that empty playground,
past childhood's sorrow,

past the past. Present.

An Old Southern Tale
To the memory of Frank Stanford

Go down in the river bottom
where the rutted, muddy road
twists into the shaded shallows
where wagons used to ford.
None but hawks and crows
will see you then (it'll be too late).
Perhaps a fox will peer
from withered, stunted shrubs,
or an ancient owl from a limb
just strong enough for wisdom
and the knowledge of death.
They'll watch you disappear
under the water's black hair,
your last words lingering
like smoke in the autumn air.

A Previously Unreported Incident

Yesterday
the sky fell
quite down
around
our ankles.
Bits of cirrus
and cumulus
clung to
our cuffs.
Careful not
to trample
astonished birds,
we craned
our necks
toward empty,
where stars
blazed gigantic.

As a Bone

I'd never say it doesn't matter;
I'd never tell that lie.
You'd know the awful truth,
that my memory stutters
every time I'm near reality
and then I'll say anything
to make the past retract
and give me back my conscience
clean and white as a bone.

Deletion

You're learning to live
with the pain.
After the first slice,
it gets easier.
A finger here,
a liver there,
and pretty soon
we're smelling
a flood of blood.
All part of the project—
the ultimate revision—
will anyone notice
all the empty you make?

Melancholia

These environs
encompass no
horizon, just
the day-to-day
play of plush light
on this window,
on that widow.
Everything

will die, it's true.
In the meantime,
this stream of rhyme
serves as sandbag
against the plash
and pull of time,
party killer,
filler with rue.

Authorities
scamper, intent
on some duties.
Lights blink on and
always back off.
She coughs into
her small, black hand,
and night slams down

on the tense town,
filled with promise,
as all towns are,
for a moment,
and then it's gone.
The rubber smiles
and random miles
march ever on.

Nebraska, May

Above us a sudden hovering,
shadow wings over corn fields.
Late spring-thaw mud sucks
on my black rubber boots.
Distance disappears to horizon
blank and bleak as this sky.
Green flies swarm the roads;
from far a screaming comes.
Souls like rain drum the dirt.

Love and Death in the Natural Order of Things

How can it be
that so much death
lives between
these moments
of senseless glee,
these snapshots
of animal joy,
spontaneous
as sex or violence?
Between each orgasm,
a graveyard fills,
bodies parting,
now departing.

Skid

I'm driving the snowy backroads drinking
a beer—irresponsible and downright
bad for a man my age (I'm thirty-nine).
But I'm not drunk; anyway, I'm thinking
that hardly anyone's on the highway.
I just needed to feel this young again,
to feel almost anything *could* happen
but nothing would, to feel that slight shimmy,
the back wheels sliding around a rare curve
on this prairie road. Is this how the spirit
feels in the face of death—like it has hit
an icy spot, lost traction, begun to swerve
into the darkening fields of winter wheat,
wheels buried to the axles in the white?

Liberation

The eyes close to the world,
but do not close.
Around us the dark rooms
in silent houses breathe.

Animals turn to flame
beneath our gaze. The wood
in tables and chairs cries out,
the metal in our refrigerator weeps

for the lost embrace of the earth.
The water in my glass trembles
in the rattle of the furnace.
How quickly the world

has shifted this morning,
how soon come out
of focus or in! We sleep
the sleep of the living,

groping with electric fingers
for the light switch
which the white wall
will not release.

Two Hours West of Tulsa

Who knew the sky flew so close to the horizon,
that the stars sang like the wind in her hair,
that the trees hung from the bluff with regret?

Who knew the words to open the mirrors,
the spells to dispel all the blues in her eyes,
to morph her sorrow into linen and light?

Who knew what questions to throw at God,
safe in our memories, sated with prayers,
yet fading into these questions we never ask?

California

The runaway truck ran down dozens in Berlin
yesterday, six days before Christmas,
an eternity before peace on earth.
A Pakistani immigrant arrested by police,
just a boy, perhaps a boy from the village I read about,
the one where seven girls were tortured to death
for dancing.

The flickering images on screens,
the flickering moments of our tiny lives
lived out in what seem like the end times,
and all I really want to do is take off
in some old muscle car, a Mustang or a GTO,
my wife by my side and old rock and roll on the radio,
heading west where the ancients believed Death
to be but where I was born what the ancients
would have considered two lifetimes ago,
when Eisenhower was president,
an era that Ginsberg condemned as fascist
but which through today's black lenses
seems merely innocent, a time of children learning
how to play together, how to unlearn
all the horrible lessons their stressed-out
and ignorant parents had taught them,
which the country in its stress and ignorance
and fear had taught them, as it bought them
with the bounty of the post-war boom,
the flight into a new kind of life that required more storage.

In those '50s: my timid, meek mother
and my pissed-off bipolar father
picking and packing citrus fruit—oranges and lemons,
grapefruit and tangerines bursting from the limbs
of the trees lined like soldiers between
the smudge pots and the boulevards,
the houses and the strip malls, fruit bright

as the blast from an A-bomb in a news reel
before the movie— "Duck and cover!"
(On my '60s school playground we added
"Kiss your ass goodbye.") The growers feared blight
but the blight was not in the fruit but in us, a lust
for more and ever more, a fear of each other
when we needed most a simple touch,
white hand to black to brown to whatever else,
a touch that burned with a need that had nothing
to do with How much? How many? Do you deliver?
but instead had everything to do with who
and where and when and why we were
and how we could get to where we knew—
just knew—we were meant to be.

Where were we? "The Inland Empire,"
San Bernardino County (and now the name
San Bernardino conjures terror, 14 dead and 22
wounded by a married couple, married to each other
but also to the ideology of terror, to Moloch the death-god),
But this was long before, and we were children
playing handball, tetherball, basketball, softball
under the steady, hazy Southern California sun,
L.A. smog settling in on the afternoons
of drowsy heat, lizard dirt, exhausted palms,
our playground huge but mostly grass-less,
hard-packed desert earth, desert kids,
Chicano and Chicana kids' families there for generations—
"We didn't cross the border, the border crossed us"—
black and white and Asian kids more recent immigrants,
white kids like me the prune pickers, children of Okies
(and the whites who streamed across
the Arizona border in the '30s and '40s were all "Okies"
from wherever), characters straight out
of The Grapes of Wrath, Woody Guthrie songs,
America's heartland from which the heart
had been ripped by wind and drought, and so
they headed west, as I still long to do,

though they were looking for work and land
and I'd be looking for something else, something
I don't yet know or realize lost as I am
in the thicket of midlife in the Midwest—
yes, in Oklahoma, an Okie but not really
because I was born in California and
have lived in two other states but mostly
different states of mind, so many states
and so many minds that I have become very confused
(are you not confused?) by the complexity,
the multiplicity, some days the difficulty of keeping
up appearances, simply drawing sufficient breath.
I think about death a lot, but not back then,
though my grandmother's death is my earliest memory
and I was fascinated by vampires sucking
the life from the veins and arteries of those of us
who thought we were living.

On the playground I was usually the last one picked
for games, the shy fat boy with the eye patch,
like an overstuffed pirate kid who couldn't hit
even a slow fastball and no parrot on my shoulder
but an owl, smart but moody, prone to secrets,
as I was prone to falling in love with girls too pretty,
too popular, to be spoken to. So I passed
my long days in the classroom where I fell in love
with words and books and several teachers
female and male and on the playground,
where I fell in love with failure, sour failure
and sweet success the two-headed Janus
coin like the one the villain Two-Face
flipped in the Batman comic books I tore through
as if they were the Talmud and I a rabbinical scholar
rather than a doughy Gentile boy
with a Jewish sense of fate born of bad brain chemistry
I suppose, all the standard woes of someone
who read too much.

Later my parents shifted from the packing plant
to shift-work in an aircraft battery factory,
assembling for Teledyne Inc. the power plants
for the F-series planes and the Hueys
and all the other expensive big-boy toys
the assembly lines of the United States
pumped out and sent to Southeast Asia,
to support and supply troops and sometimes rain
fire on people who looked to me somewhat
like a few of the kids in the cafeteria
where we had fish every Friday, tostadas regularly,
and the perennial celery sticks with peanut butter,
white or chocolate milk, don't forget to put your trays
on the belt or you'll be in trouble.

I lived in a bubble then,
and one year it burst, popped
like a stretched-out sphere of air and gum:
the first and only fight my parents
ever had in front of me, my mother's heart attack,
my father's nervous breakdown,
the flag-draped coffins and Walter Cronkite's
calm report of casualties every evening
on the CBS news, the explosion across the street
when the teenaged revolutionary's pipe bomb
blew his hands off in his parents' basement.

Every summer since I could remember
we'd packed a few things in my father's blue
and white Chevrolet Fleetside pickup
with the camper shell and headed east on I-40,
the old Route 66, reversing the Okies' trek,
across the Mojave with its brutal blankness
and dust, through Gallup and Tucumcari
and the mesas of New Mexico, stopping
at Stuckey's for gas and sandwiches
and if I was lucky some candy,
towards Amarillo ("Eat this 72-ounce steak

dinner in one hour and it's free")
and western Oklahoma's wheat fields
and oil fields, to where my dad was from, to family.

But this time we packed everything,
and we left California forever, and I left
my childhood forever in the orange groves
and the dry wash of the Santa Ana River,
in the classrooms and on the playgrounds
of Lugonia Elementary, in Dodger Stadium echoing
Vin Scully's voice from tinny transistor radios,
left it behind me like a snake's shed skin,
on my way to become what I've become,
somewhere else, in these many states
and many minds.

The Metaphysics of Prairie

The roads here are so straight
sometimes you think
you'll just keep going forever,
until you see water
in the distance,
and think eventually
you'll run right into it
and drive to another continent
somewhere far, far away

Everything here is straight lines,
everything is horizon.
It's no wonder people here
think the way they do.
It's very linear here

But often, in the distance . . .
I'm not sure if it's clouds
or a haze of some sort,
but there's a grayness hanging
over the horizon,
a sense of uncertainty,
a question mark
suspended over the prairie,
and I know then it's all an illusion,
that it's not really straight,
but there's a subtle, so subtle curve,

and that eventually
I'll drive to, not an illusion,
but simply more prairie,
until I arrive back at the very
same place:
the period under the curve.

Pineapples

Stumbling, stuttering, vacant and lost,
the old man with the Billy-goat beard
and the 15-gallon straw cowboy hat
cut through the crowd of consumers
at the Wichita shopping mall
like a machete through a pineapple
in an old South Seas survival film,
one that the old man had seen often
as a child at the now-closed cinema
downtown by the Harley dealer,
where one of the dudes has a similar beard
and a fondness for blades and forbidden fruit,
though pineapple is forbidden only by fools
who've never been to the Oahu roadside stands
where the old man with the beard and hat
used to take his girlfriend for a treat
after a long day of snorkeling, making love
before his Naval hitch ended and she stayed
and he returned home to the aircraft plant
and his high school sweetie who'd broken his heart,
that same sweetie who died giving birth
to a daughter who died later that day,
and he started in with pineapple juice and rum
but soon shucked all pretense, all decorum,
and took to the thick strong wine
straight from the brown bagged bottle
until he couldn't keep anything in one piece
and bit by jagged bit he burst apart
though that bursting took twenty years
and this morning he went to the mall
for no reason, no reason at all,
and walked its sweetly-tiled length
until the security guards ran him out at closing
and he sat down in the empty parking lot
and watched the bright moon over Wichita
turn slowly to the ripest of pineapples.

In the Kiamichis

Swerving the sweet mountain road
sun high in your mirror shaded eyes
you suddenly hear music
a minor key in your ears
blues jumping up like grasshoppers
into your quiet mind
so you slow and pull over
in a meadow filled
with Black-Eyed Susans
and try to train your brain
on some little things
her lisp when excited
the bright flash of her words
early on an autumn morning
yes some little things
like lines from old songs
playing through your head
in a field full of nothing
beside a mountain road

Oklahoma Panhandle

By day the sun revels in the fields,
the sky shimmers in the sticky heat,
and the brown children play
in the respite of morning breeze.

This land is bloated with bones,
nameless things sunk in the muck of time,
irrigated by red rivers pumping
from old wounds deep within the earth.

At night the moon broods too closely.
You feel you're at the bottom of a bowlful of stars
about to brim over into the heart of something
hidden just beneath the world.

Mentone, California, 1969

I stood alone, as usual,
under the late-afternoon sun,
baseball bat slung over my sloping shoulder,
watching the clouds' shadows
shifting through the orange groves,
smell of the ripening fruit
igniting inside me.
In that moment I knew
I was unusually alone—
Mom and Dad never to return,
houses along the cul-de-sac
suddenly empty, abandoned,
not even a bird in the hot July sky—
it was the first day
of my life as the sole survivor
of I would never know what,
so I tossed a ball into the air,
drove a line drive toward the fragrant tree line,
an heroic crack no one would ever hear.

The Woman at the Port Angeles Cemetery
For Tess Gallagher and the late Raymond Carver

Waiting with her floral head scarf and jangling bracelets,
she'd seem more at home in a gypsy caravan
were it not for the shine in her almond-colored eyes.

She stands alone in this beautiful garden of stones
near the ocean, clearly visible through a wide break
in a stand of towering evergreens.

Her name is on the right, his on the left--
certainly no political symbolism there--
in between, his favorite photo of the two of them

smiling like foolish lovers, which they were,
into a future filled with possibilities, which weren't,
in those too-short days before the surgery.

Don't speak to her; leave her alone.
Don't make inane comments about the weather.
This is Seattle, and of course it will rain.

Just go away and leave them alone,
he in his black bed beneath the stone,
she in her bright defiant mourning dress.

Lizard King
For Jim Morrison, wherever he may be

You stare from your frame
on my wall, dead man,
a fretful cigarette
smoldering in your swollen hand,
and you're the spitting image
of someone preparing to die.

I bought you
in a shady stall
along the Seine
on a too-warm March day,
mellow on Prozac and vin rouge,
on my way to Shakespeare & Company.

Don't you just hate poems about Europe,
like all those '50s formalists
writing sonnets about Roman fountains
while McCarthy turned artists
on the spit of his blindness
and advisers infiltrated Saigon?

Let's just say I was in Paris
after visiting your grave
and wanted to stay there with you,
because at home an unelected president
sharpened his bloody knives to sacrifice sons and fathers,

mothers and daughters,
so we wouldn't notice
the swelling trust funds,
the stench of rotting rhetoric
as the tanks rolled toward Baghdad,
and I was ashamed of America.

You're bloated and haggard, Jim,
because you'd given up by then:
blood in the streets, Nixon triumphant,
your words spinning away
in the booze and sex and cigarettes
and all you wanted was to be Rimbaud.

I look at you and realize you'd be old now.
But you'd still be here,
not moldering in dirt and memories.
You remind me what not to become,
that the bastards can't—won't—win,
that even poems about Europe
sometimes lead us home.

On Sparrowhawk Mountain

Through Oklahoma hills
the river rolls below the rocky point,
cold and green in the thick spring.
Old leaves crackle,
slipping under lovers' feet.

Gouged into stone, names stare:
    J.K. + S.T.,
    Sigmas #1,
    Jesus is Love,
so many words massed here,
simple, senseless joys
falling all over one another,
layers of lust and God
beneath so much sky.

Fish slide through the heavy waters.
Under pale clumps of clouds
a sparrowhawk hovers
against the sun,
feathers of light in its eyes.

Pastoral

The sunrise over Tulsa
glimpsed above the red roof
of the drowsy Quick Trip—
today has possibilities,
though none as exciting
as the fast-receding past
where you were once younger
than your children are now.

There's no Pope in Rome,
where the sad birds spiral
blindly over St. Peter's dome,
and only the little old nuns
who've known only hope
walk through the afternoon
with faces bright as God's.

Here in middle America
pickup trucks crowd the spaces
in the Best Western parking lot.
A middle-aged chambermaid
mutters Hindi to herself as
she labors at the stairs.

Your wife waits for a plane.
You watch the sunrise, and imagine
those spiraling Italian birds,
dancing the currents of the sky
staring blindly there as here.

Florence, 2015

Imagine Michelangelo
in skinny jeans
and a soccer shirt
jostling tourists
outside Il Duomo
on his way to
Paradiso, all
marble, chisels,
sweat and dust,
light sudden
as a white dove
above Brunelleschi's
red dome
pointed to
by the crowds.

Travelogue

They give you no maps,
only the vaguest of directions.
"Somewhere that-a-way," they say,
snickering under their tattered breaths
at your considerable confusion.
So on and on and on you go,
shoe leather, tires, hair wearing thin,
debts and pounds accumulating,
'til finally you're barefoot, sunburned,
the odometer's broken,
but you know no life but motion
so on and on and on you go,
to the valley of dry, brittle bones.

Fame, Fame, Fame, Fame

Today is the birthday
of someone so famous
we've forgotten her name.
Or is it his name
we've forgotten, along
with nationality,
place of birth, baptismal records,
eye and hair color, height and weight,
the spaces between the mysterious teeth,
the peculiar way the eyes roamed
if left alone for even a minute,
the habit of surreptitiously devouring dirt,
the identical skirts and jackets
hanging like souls in a darkened walk-in,
the diary filled with pages blank
save for an infinitesimal *I*
in the lower-left corner of each?

As in Certain Paintings of Paul Klee

Cartoonish bubbly hands clawing
through a thick quilt of color,
patches glowing with pigmented light.
This thin world slowly resolves itself
into an order fit for a child—
one hand, one finger, one table, one fish—
these luminous, shockingly heavy things
with which we weight down our hearts
to hold them tight within our chests.
Outside the window morning is grey,
dull birds desolately circling the sky.
Within this frame, we wriggle our toes
in the blue grass in one corner,
poking our fears into fat black brushstrokes
that separate us from our nightmares,
the pale despairs of unpainted canvases.

Cinema Noir

Always a lady killer, the man in black
    holds a belladonna bouquet
        choked with white ribbon.

Katherine doesn't know
    he knows where she lives,
        what she feels at night

alone with faded paperbacks
    and a short-stemmed glass
        of cool white wine.

Her friend waltzes
    in the shadows with a man
        with a black boutonniere.

She will die soon,
    horribly, but mercifully off-screen.
        She had it coming

because she was the friend,
    because she knew too much
        she didn't know she knew.

The drunken detective's wife is dead
    killed by the man whose breath
        smelled of garlic and roses.

Don't worry. Simply
    eat your popcorn and pretend
        it'll come out all right in the end.

The reels will spin around all night.
Everyone who deserves to die will.

Blank Document

And there you have it,
two words tormenting
in their willful challenge,
sassy and streetwise
beyond their limited
number of characters,
cocksure, strutting,
very much in your face,
Ace, turn up the bass
and hand over
the damned microphone,
you're about to be schooled
in the fine old-time art
of saying nothing (for,
really, what's left?) but
making it sound so good
the pixels cling to the page
in something very much
like love, like meaning,
like a momentary, though
fragmentary, stay.

Picasso Kite

It's like that, you know.
Everything's a project,
and we're all just projectors
of whatever filmy emotion we feel
on those or these particular days
of wine and roses, profound neuroses,
feelings like the project
my son once made
that I always call the Picasso Kite
because that's what it looks like
and I love self-expression,
depression, negation,
like this project
which started out as a poem
but became a mere draft
under the closed door
through minute cracks in the floor
which isn't really solid enough
to hold the weight of the world
which as it winds down
begins to resemble
in some reassembled way
a project made
by a bored child at play.

Them Blues

Easy enough, at times, to believe this is the devil's music.
What else would Lucifer listen to in hell
but, over and over, twelve bars of joyful tragedy,
triumphant, shouting, ecstatic pain
well worth selling most souls for?
Drums and bass lock into the beat
and just don't ever let go,
while the guitar writhes and moans,
bottleneck slide scraping steel strings
into something unholy, as far from a simple strum
as the fiery pit is from streets of gold.
And the singer's story is always the same:
lover gone bad, mule gone lame,
money all lost in a poker game,
the slambam facts of life on a fallen earth.
But the way she or he sings it,
you just know that no one's allowed to give up,
that checking out early is not an option,
that this song has to go on and on
until Judgment Day, until the very end of time.
So Satan and I sit back and tap talons and toes
to Robert Johnson, Son House, Howlin' Wolf,
Koko Taylor, Muddy Waters, and B. B. King,
'cause when you're down
ain't nothing left to do but sing.

Alzheimer's
To the memory of Omegia Blanch Hornbuckle Stinson

I know I know I used to know your name;
you lived in that thing atop the hill,
up there, way up there,
behind those towers where the birds sit
and sing in my head all day.
These people come, every night,
and we watch TV, and I'm afraid.
I don't know I don't know I used to know their names.
In the morning they make me swallow pills—
white, yellow, blue, and pink.
Why are pills never black like the sun,
or that other color, you know, the one like my eyes?
My house, if that's what it really is,
festers with photographs
full of strangers' faces and smiles,
oddly shaped children with huge heads and hands,
mouths full of frightening teeth.
I know I don't know I just can't remember
this woman who hides in my mirror.

Life Insurance

When we first met, I knew
the world was sane, at least
for a little while, since
it moved on its axis just enough
to slide you toward me.

Now, nothing is safe anymore:
planes fall from the sky
on kindergartens,
radiation seeps from
our shower heads,
tornadoes pick apart
the remnants of our lives.

Strangers with black eyes
break into our houses,
dissect our families,
carve their initials
into our children,
melt back into the abyss.

What a time to try
to be human--
with so much so jagged,
so bitter,
how much it means
to taste your salty flesh,
to move into you in the night
once more, and again,
and forever.

Mors Praematura
To the memory of Elizabeth Thompson Roberts

There's money on the bed, but it's no good here.
Paris outside my window shrugs its shoulders, says "Non."
I see not a single bird among these foreign branches.

At Notre Dame yesterday I longed to confess something
to the fat priest holding so many guilty tongues,
but the line outside grew pilgrims by the minute.

So I lit a candle for you, Beth, and sent a prayer
up to the stained glass holding the Virgin
tight in the agnostic tourists' camera lenses

and thought how we're all agnostics
when we're so far away from home
and the light hits our skin so brightly

we can almost see our blood moving
along these gray worm-like veins, wriggling
along toward our fucking lonesome, too-sad hearts.

You named your children William and Mary,
ironic choices for a Catholic convert who knew
how history offers such violent usurpations,

how one learns patience only through laughter
and both the best and worst kinds of great love,
and how both are the opposite ends of the candle

I want to believe is somehow still burning
long after the priest assigns his final "Our Father"
and the heavy doors close on all living and dead.

Paris, May 2014

Sawdust Man
To the memory of William Cris Stinson

Now, father, when I think of you,
I think most often of sawdust—
fine, sandy grainings of the stuff
sifting down my collar, my arms,
pooling at the base of my spine.
Together we slaughtered forests,
fashioned boards into makeshift barns,
sawed, planed, sanded, hammered in place.
And all the time you coughed and swore,
sputtered and raged, and I looked on
with the son's sad, detached concern.
Oh most imperfect carpenter—
shall we never again approach
those trembling trees with saws in hand,
never again inhale their flesh
and from their muscles build a son?

The Something Else

Listen: I remember—
we were watching Halley's Comet
crawl lamely across the sky.

And you predicted we'd
be together to see it again.
But the odds don't look good.

The nights are too soft now,
the days too bright,
edges drawn with felt tips;

I feel I'm breathing through gauze.
Then suddenly I see a star fall,
and I remember a harder night,

us lying on a gravel beach,
bottle of tequila passing between us,
and the something else

you simply couldn't swallow,
that vow you tried to memorize,
but never did. That night

the crickets' legs scraped
in rhythm to the blood in our veins
but nothing held together;

the moment flowed away,
dissipated in the black wind.
So, look: the stars stay

content in their places,
the wind blows nothing
but night, and

the crickets simply wait
for something that passes
with the first light of dawn.

On Three Hats of My Father's

My father's checkered, hounds toothed hats
festoon the top of my tallest bookshelf,
higher than any other art or ornament
in this untidy, idea-crowded office
save the token cheap medieval crucifix
I liberated from Westminster Abbey.
He'll never need those silly hats again;
earth and stone now shade his head.
And, as he always said, mine's too large
to wear those brightly patterned lids,
the quaint ugly kind that old men wear
on those seemingly never-ending days
when they wander the empty winter beaches
wondering what's to become of their sons.

At the Gospel Singing

My father sings and taps his foot,
words soar in summer air,
salvation songs, damnation songs,
how we'll all meet up there,
that happy land that he'll see by
and by. I sit beside
him on the pew we've shared for years,
and try hard to decide

why God makes fools of all of us.
I only feel the sweat
that pools upon my lower back,
the penitent wood, and heat.
I hold a recorder in my hand.
He'll play the hymns for years,
for an eternity. He'll play
them loudly when he hears

my feet fall on his creaking porch,
the prodigal come home
from wandering in the wilderness
from which no good could come.
He'll pour hot coals upon my head
and have me fetch a cup.
He'll smile above his Maxwell House
and turn the volume up.

But now he sways, eyes tightly closed,
and sings the gospel truth.
He seems to feel; I can't be sure.
can just God be enough?
The sound that flees his mouth is cool,
so clear it cleans the air
around us; I see angels fly
and shake my head and stare

at the good man who gave me life
but whom I've never known.
He followed Jesus up the hill
while I sat out alone
and found the peace of being lost
to find my own way out.
My road has led me to this church—
to Father, Son, and Doubt.

Never Pills

Colors of Good & Plenty—
a candy I hated—pink and white
but melded into one capsule
my father swallowed with an OJ nightcap
right before he removed his dentures.

I never learned the word lithium
until much later. They were "nerve pills,"
and years later I found a note
my father had written
where he referred to "never pills,"

and that seemed right. He never
quite fit in, but the pills
made the awkward fits a little less so.
Laughter and anger smoothed and roughed
the edges of the boxes he (we) found ourselves in.

I dislike the term mental illness
as I dislike the word depression.
I prefer madness, melancholy, as I am a romantic.
I have read too much. Perhaps I have lived too much.
I know he felt that way, yet he hung on,

his mind slowly calming
after the years of rages,
broken furniture and fingers,
profane tirades, long sullen withdrawals
into the "pouting house,"

the cabin where he exiled himself,
listening for hours
to old Southern gospel songs
from his Arkansas Baptist childhood
echoing off the plain walls,

living on peanut butter and orange juice
and nerve pills until he could bear
to be a husband, a father again.
I would lie: "I know how he felt."
I cannot.

I inherited only the melancholy,
the withdrawing side, but without the faith
(though with the desperate need for it).
Mania's not my style, but I can be sad
with the worst of them/us/me/you.

He's been gone 16 years now,
and still I feel him inside me
each and every day. Perhaps
the pink side of the pills was his soft side,
the sensitive side that terrified him,

raised as he was in a river bottom
scrabbling for crumbs from rocky land,
raised to be hard, to kill to eat,
to subdue nature rather than enjoy it.
Yet he would take time

to watch the breeze rustle the grass,
the sunlight filter through the trees,
and he would sigh. He
didn't know I heard him,
but I did.

The white side of the pills
was the blankness.
If you're reading this poem,
you probably know about that.
Don't you?

Sometimes

Sometimes an orange football rolling across the floor.
Sometimes a sycamore, thrusting its barren branches
                                    into the winter sky.

Sometimes a small white dog, yapping through
                                    a colorblind dream.
Sometimes a documentary on Andy Warhol playing unwatched
                                    in a room full of people.

Sometimes they're the wrong people.
Sometimes you are.
Sometimes all of us agree to just be sad together.
Sometimes we can't stop.

Sometimes things move in the corners of my eyes
and I hear choirs of sexless angels.
Sometimes I'm a sexless angel
and I'm singing and I move
in the corners of someone's eyes.

Sometimes the world's a scratched record
and the needle's leaping,
and heaven's in its landings.
Sometimes I think I'm dying

more quickly than usual,
and I buy myself flowers.
Sometimes I see God

hiding in the tiny spaces
between these words, between our bodies.

Agnostic Stanzas

Woke this morning ignorant
as the day I was born,
brittle bone colander in my head.

Hundreds died yesterday in the name of certainty
though x ≠ y; it doesn't always even = x.
Physicists propose another Earth, in a universe we cannot
see.

In that world, painters portray the Devil
as an old white man with flowing beard
bearing a banner emblazoned in red "No Doubts."

Of Winter and Ordinary Time

The sycamores haunt me,
bleached branches
like dead gods' bones
flung into starry nothing.

Holy Mary, Mother of God,
forgive us our belief,
as we forgive our doubt.

Wine and bread weren't enough,
so I chose fine white cheese
and a thin slice of silence,
the breathing of the dead.

Bless us, Oh, Lord,
and these thy gifts,
bruised and broken as they be.

A Matter of Fact
To the memory of Carson McCullers

Nothing tonight
about the sky,
no ode to moon
or brazen wind.
Nature died
in 1989 but
no one noticed.

Mobile lumps
of tainted clay
lumber through
what remains,
sifting the ashes
in a pathetic
search for god.

A vague rumor,
urban legend
lurking often
in the corners
of consciousness,
God was a tree,
a rock, a cloud.

One Reason the Agnostic Still Prays

At the bottom of her life,
where she had lain down to die,
she saw no stars above.
The earth held her tenuously,
waiting to fold her in.
Her mouth sewn shut,
her eyes stared, dry.
She was numb as a stone.

To her dark left
something spread awful wings.
To her right, dim as clear water,
a delicate bell rang, once only.
She'd say something pulled her up,
but she can't so truthfully lie.
No white lights or tongues of fire—
she just didn't want to be there anymore.

On the Eastern Front

So what to begin with—
the mortars that a failed memory
keeps fusillading over our walls,

walls we've prayed would hold
back the infernal barbarians
with their lustful, crack toothed leers,

leers we ourselves have borrowed
on occasion from the fogged mirrors
where our faces appear like stones

erupting from the black surface of a lake,
lake where large mysteries swim
through waters glacially chilled,

waters the war canoes rip through
on their way to the expanding front,
where nomadic children maddened

by the just, harsh poverty of God
line up the lovely silver shells
like verses from the sorrowful, sacred book

Winter Solo

Sunday after Epiphany the world
has been quieted in January ice.
The roads are too slick to drive to church,
so I walk through the silent cold
of this sleepy town to buy newspapers.
I see no cars, no dogs, no birds, but tracks
of animal and man cover the white ground.
I think of those preachers from my childhood
who told of the rapture, how the faithful
would be caught up in the sky with the Lord,
leaving the faithless behind. Today's like that,
as if I were the only sinner wandering
through a town evacuated by God.
A cruising police car reassures me I'm not alone;
it's not the end of time, just the beginning
of a week in winter's darkest month.
At home my wife is still burrowed in bed,
trying to sleep while the children
watch TV and eat Captain Crunch and ask
again and again if they can build a snowman,
though there's little snow, only cold and ice.
Here in this little Oklahoma town I call home
I and all the world wait silently for a revelation,
like the ice melting on the young, green wheat,
the flower tip pushing its way through the dirt,
a stone of cold doubt heavily rolling
away from the open mouth of an empty tomb.

Winter Solstice 2016

Now—only four days before Christmas, and people appear
in short-sleeved shirts after the longest freeze so far this year,
and the sunshine filters through the kinds of clouds Monet loved,
sclera-colored, diffuse as the mind's thoughts on such a day—
the first day of winter. Outside the outlet mall I sit in my car,
waiting for two of those I love to pick out a winter coat
in case the calendar recalls the season.

Cards, signs, and online posts exhort us to remember
"the reason for the season," and I of course know what they mean,
being raised to believe in such things, but I believe the reason
is that it's the shortest day of the year, a day of scant and fleeting light
before the fall of darkness, and our ancestors recognized
the sky's signs in a way we have forgotten and knew that after this day
things would be different for many weeks.

Things *will* be different soon, with a president whom a majority
of Americans rejected assuming the highest office, and we the people
divided in a scary kind of way I can't remember since the '60s,
when I was just a kid and the world seemed filled with wonder and hope.

56

But I walked through the mall earlier, enjoying the sun, the snatches
of Spanish and Arabic and Vietnamese smattering through
our twangy English, everyone united

in their search for gifts for those they love, those they like, those
they feel connected to whether they wish to be or not,
fashionably-dressed people, slim and chic, already wearing
the brands of the stores they filter in and out of, looking marvelous,
magical as the day, while old shabby men like me who care little
for fashion sit in the sun like lizards on rocks, some smoking,
some talking bowl games, all waiting for their loves.

Perhaps it was the sun in my eyes—bright even through my shades—
but I thought I saw Walt Whitman scribbling in a notebook
among the smart phone tappers, smiling benevolence on the Americans
around him—the children of immigrants now speaking fluent English
to their children, fluent Spanish to their parents, the two slim young boys
with brightly dyed hair and ear studs strolling hand in hand
amongst the shoppers, oblivious in their love to the few stares,

the old white couple staring, scared to see a love like theirs
in such a combination, the black family with the two small boys—
so vulnerable, so threatened, yet so vibrant in their youth—
conversing about the lunch options in the food court. And
my stomach rumbles, though not with hunger, rather
with a sudden love for this, all *this*, in its ordinariness,
Its stubborn refusal of fear, of dread

of what the next year may bring, of the chaotic din
of the news and the streets and the minds of so many citizens.
And I know I must love this world, as you must,
as long as it is ours, as long as it stands, on this—
the solstice of our aching, yearning hearts.

Fog

I meant to type "Fog" just now but at first I typed "Gof," and that made me think of God,
    which I do
a lot since I turned 50 and decided I'm an agnostic in love with ritual, tradition, a sense of
    community,
which of course I know I could find perhaps in masonry or falconry or martial arts or the
    Republican Party
which I don't believe in because in my mind G.O.P. stands for "Greedy Old People," and I'm not
    old and I'm not greedy,
just needy like most people nowadays or maybe—maybe—always, people needing each other's
    support
to validate their existences and choices, like the choices we make at Wal-Mart which I love to
    hate
and hate to love because they've driven out of business all those mom-and-pop stores in all those
    quaint little downtowns,
you know, the shops with nothing much and you paid a whole lot for nothing much, but at least
    they'd make eye contact
while they checked you out—I mean your merchandise, not you—which is more than I can say
    for the tired middle-aged women
with the carpal tunnel-related casts on their varicose wrists who are too weary to say "Hi" when
    I go through
with my dog food, staple guns, tampons, and grapefruit, my diet pills and Rocky Road (and isn't
    every road rocky in the end?).

Wait. I was talking about God, wasn't I?

Black and Green
For Lawrence Ferlinghetti & to the memory of Johnny Cash

For 100 days that seem a decade
we've been somnambulist tightrope walkers
barefoot and pregnant with dread
feet bleeding from the wires
stretching between November 8 and now.
We often wear black upon our backs
in mourning for those who've fallen,
rounded up like sheep, corralled, deported,
denied reentry, censored, shamed,
thrown under the red-white-and-blue bus
powered by 100% American fossil fuels.
We clearly see so little–
distant lights where futures might be
waiting for all of us clowns
and ragtag, vagabond performers
teetering on so many sharp edges,
catching each other and holding on like Hell
then slowly moving onward, propped and ready
for another show, more doom-defiant acts,
making every single one of our selves matter.

Mirrors
Inspired by Adrienne Rich's "Dedications"

I know who you are
sitting in the back of the squad car,
bruised, cracked ribs beginning to throb,
beaten, busted for walking while black
on the burning streets of Bakersfield.

I know who you are
gritting your teeth in the grocery
just off the Pine Ridge rez
as the blonde clerk eyes your braids
and says the SNAP reader is down
as you are pulling bills from your wallet
to pay for your son's cough syrup.

I know who you are
walking toward the Youth Shelter
on South Madison in Tulsa
after your Baptist daddy kicked you out
when he found you with that other boy,
the one whose hair you somehow still smell
even after weeks on the streets.

I know who you are
popping another pain pill
because every part of you hurts
from the trauma of being lost
in the midst of your home town,
hard by the boarded-up factory
where all your people had labored.

I know who you are
running out the back
as ICE agents storm the front.
Your two sisters disappeared
from Juarez, you can't go there.

You'll drown yourself in the Rio Grande
if they deport you, drown the baby
in your belly to save her
from joining your sisters
in their oblivious desert graves.

I know who you are
watching as old wealthy men
say we can't afford to insure you,
they need their tax cuts
more than you need to live.
Just go to the local E.R.
where all the other poor people
go to die, or somehow survive
until the next late-night visit
you can never afford.

I know who you are
waking in the night
from dreams of Mosul, 2014,
your best friend blown up
while eating lunch
in the base dining hall—
one minute laughing from across
the room, waving you over,
the next gone, like your arm,
leaving jagged fragments
forever lodged in your body and brain.

I know who you are
as I know who I am,
more fortunate than you
but also frightened
by who we have all become—
sheep and wolves,
sometimes both the same day,

the same old way of prey and killer,
diverting ourselves with fake news and perversion,
waiting for the world to change
so we won't have to.

I know you. You know me.
I see your faces in my mirror,
faces of empathy and indifference,
defiance and resignation,
understanding and confusion.
Let the moment last. Keep looking
for—say—four years.
Wipe the glass with our millions of hands,
clear the fog, remain steady.
Whatever else we do, remain.

64% of a Sonnet on the Eternal Theme

The tree that strangely stares at me
from across the addled alley
surely holds within its withered bark
no lingering malice, though regret
may be sometimes seen
when it ponders its fallen leaves,
limbs stacked against its old trunk
for a windless, cool spring day
and the inevitable burning.

Rising Green

whisper
you will
please yourself
ultimately

if you only listen
to the rain
washing
the sun away

slowly
behind your back
the shadow
stretches and leaps

too quickly
for the shaman
to learn
any of his tricks

Vegetation

No, no one saw you.
I'm quite sure of that.
Your secret is safe
for another night.
Breathe easier now.

Plant your rank sins deep,
water them with tears.
In time they may sprout,
spread out across you,
vines with blood-red blooms.

Tighter

Green moments in a great day—
the liftoff of the morning's light
falling into your upturned face,
the sprinkle of rain around noon
that settled the restive dust,
redbirds' feathers reflecting rays
filtering through the maple leaves.

Such moments tend to escape.
Hold them tightly. Tighter.

Memory Upon Waking

Gracefully they move
through the rooms of the sky
stepping off the clouds
soaring diving without wings
in the corners of the wind
skimming over where I stand
watching, feet heavy as sin,
grounded in the wild-eyed
moment of this dream.

Bipolar

I woke up one winter
with your nerves on my throat,
sadness in my nostrils.
Outside the chill windows
the birds fought one another
with almost-human ferocity,
and the naked branches sang
Hebraic chants for the dead.
"Well, hell," I said, and arose.

For after all, it was Friday,
quiet, warm as a house.
The limited possibilities
were quite *there* nonetheless.
When I touched my loose skin
I remembered only your hands.
Outside me, the dead leaves
gyred upwards on the wind,
grasped the cold branches, greened.

Don Stinson studied creative writing at Northeastern State University and Oklahoma State University and has taught writing and literature for over 20 years at Northern Oklahoma College, where with colleagues he organizes the annual Chikaskia Literary Festival. His poems have been published by many regional and national literary magazines and websites, and he has read his work at festivals and conferences around the U. S. He and his wife Pamela live in Tonkawa but travel widely.

www.ingramcontent.com/pod-product-compliance
Lightning Source LLC
Chambersburg PA
CBHW020958090426
42736CB00010B/1370